Emmy Noether, A Woman of Greatness

by

Marcia Bohn

First published by AuthorHouse 06/28/05

ISBN: 1-4208-5305-8 (sc)

Printed in the United States of America
Bloomington, Indiana

This book is printed on acid-free paper.

authorHOUSE

1663 LIBERTY DRIVE
BLOOMINGTON, INDIANA 47403
(800) 839-8640
www.authorhouse.com

This book is dedicated to Dyanne Tracy, a phenomenal professor at Oakland University in Michigan, who had a significant impact on the way I teach math. She taught me to enjoy math instead of being afraid of it. Thank you, Dr. Tracy!

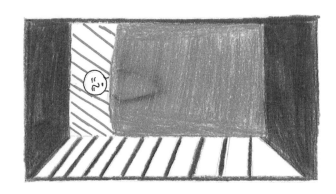

A long time ago, a great woman named Emmy Noether was born in a town called Erlangen. Erlangen was in a country called Germany.

Emmy's family was part of a religion called Judaism. Emmy was the oldest child in her family.

She had three younger
brothers, but only
one of them lived.

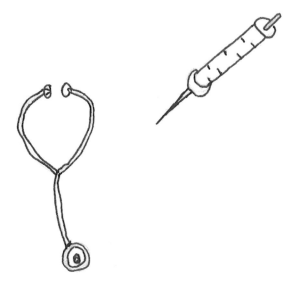

This was because, back then, doctors didn't have all the new things to help people like they do now.

Emmy was very near-sighted
throughout her whole life
and wore thick glasses
to help her see better.

Emmy loved math, but she knew that she could never get a job using math because women weren't allowed to learn math.

She learned skills that were important for girls of her time to have.

She learned how to play the clavier, which is sort of like a piano. She also cooked and dusted.

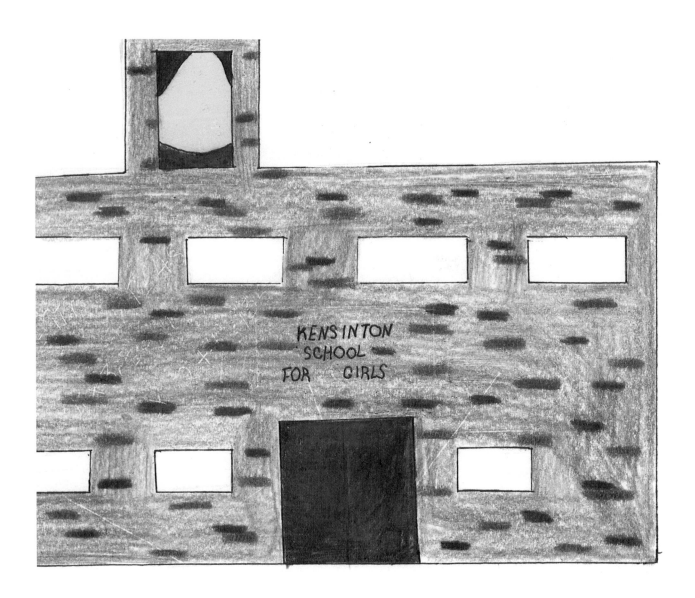

Emmy went to school and studied French and English. After high school, she became certified to teach in schools for girls.

Emmy wasn't satisfied with this, though. She sat in on classes at college with her brother, Fritz.

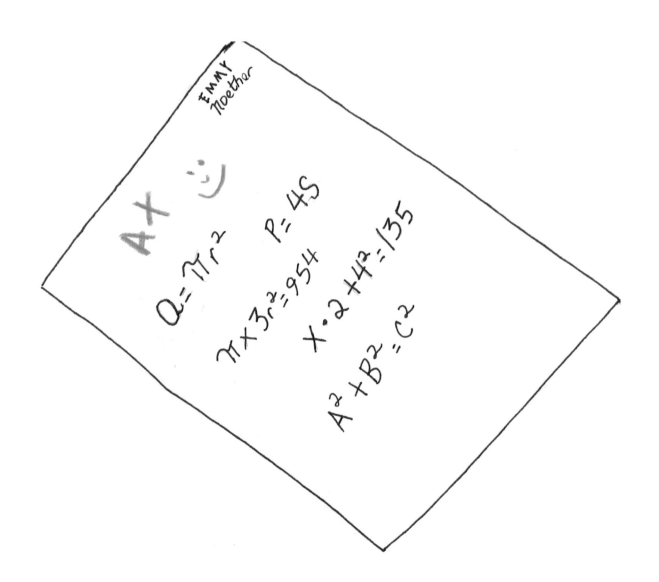

Two years later, she took an exam to enter the math program at the University of Erlangen and passed!

Five years later, she received her degree!

Emmy still wasn't happy. No one wanted to hire a woman.

For the next ten years, Emmy worked without pay at a math school in Erlangen.

In 1919, two great mathematicians heard about Emmy. They invited her to teach at their university in Gottingen. Gottingen is also in Germany. Emmy still wasn't paid for her work.

Three years later, though, she did receive a small salary for her work.

Emmy stayed at the university until 1933 when a man named Adolf Hitler gained power in Germany.

He demanded that all Jewish people be thrown out of all university positions.

Emmy moved to America
because some friends
had found a job for her
at a women's college in
Philadelphia called Bryn Mawr.

OLD
WORLD

NEW
WORLD

Emmy loved her job in America! She felt like she was living in another world!

Emmy's boss understood how she was feeling and tried to make her feel at home.

Emmy would often take her students out for Saturday afternoon walks. She would think so hard about math that she would forget about traffic, and her students would have to protect her.

Emmy taught with greatness and made lasting impressions on her students at Bryn Mawr.

Emmy loved Bryn Mawr and taught there until she died in 1935.

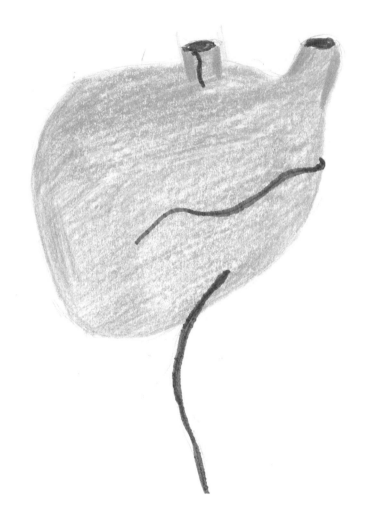

Emmy didn't let anyone know that she was sick, and one day her heart wasn't strong enough to keep working so it stopped.

Emmy's death was a shock
to all her friends and family.

After her death, her Russian friend, Alexandroff, said, "Emmy Noether was the greatest of women mathematicians, a great scientist, an amazing teacher, and an unforgettable person!"

The following is a list of words that may be troublesome for the young readers of this book:

Erlangen—A town in Germany. This is where Emmy grew up.

Germany—A country far from the United States. This should be introduced because children of the age group that this book is written for may not have any concept of life or people outside of their own town, let alone life outside of their own state or country.

Judaism—A type of religion such as Catholicism or Protestantism. This was Emmy's religion.

Near-sighted—This is a word used by eye doctors to refer to people that cannot see things very well that are far away.

Clavier—A musical instrument that resembles a piano.

References

Noether, Gottfried. *Emmy Noether, Women of Mathematics, A Biobibliographic Sourcebook.* (Greenwood Press, 1987).

Perl, Teri. *Women and Numbers.* (Wide World Publishing/Tetra, 1993).

Perl, Teri. *Women in Mathematics, Lives in Women Mathematicians* (Wide World Publishing, 1993).

Taussky-Todd, Olga. (1985). <u>Autobiographical Essay,</u> "Mathematical People, and Profiles and Interviews." Chicago: Contemporary.

Lightning Source UK Ltd.
Milton Keynes UK
UKIC01n0053140415
249582UK00009B/66

9 781420 853056